DRAW YOUR DAY

FOR Kids!

HOW TO SKETCH AND PAINT YOUR AMAZING LIFE

BY SAMANTHA DION BAKER

CROWN BOOKS FOR YOUNG READERS ♛ NEW YORK

*For Ian and Theo, who make my world brighter,
make me laugh daily, and inspire me to draw my days.*

All rights reserved. Published in the United States by
Crown Books for Young Readers, an imprint of Random House Children's Books,
a division of Penguin Random House LLC, New York.

Crown and the colophon are registered trademarks of Penguin Random House LLC.

Visit us on the Web! rhcbooks.com

Educators and librarians, for a variety of teaching tools,
visit us at RHTeachersLibrarians.com

Library of Congress Cataloging-in-Publication Data
Names: Baker, Samantha Dion, author.
Title: Draw Your Day for Kids! : How to Sketch and Paint your
Amazing Life / by Samantha Dion Baker.
Description: First edition. | New York : Crown Books for Young Readers, [2021] |
Audience: Ages 8–12 | Audience: Grades 3–7 | Summary: "The kid's version of popular
Instagram artist Samantha Dion Baker's *Draw Your Day,* an instructive
and inspirational guide to keeping a daily sketch journal"— Provided by publisher.
Identifiers: LCCN 2021007889 (print) | LCCN 2021007890 (ebook) |
ISBN 978-0-593-37890-8 (trade paperback) | ISBN 978-0-593-37891-5 (ebook)
Subjects: LCSH: Drawing—Themes, motives—Juvenile literature. |
Drawing—Authorship—Juvenile literature.
Classification: LCC NC715 .B353 2021 (print) | LCC NC715 (ebook) | DDC 741.2—dc23

The text of this book is set in 10-point Gotham Rounded.
The illustrations in this book were created using mixed media.

MANUFACTURED IN SINGAPORE
10 9 8 7 6 5 4 3 2 1
First Edition

CONTENTS

PART ONE   WHY DRAW YOUR DAY?   1

PART TWO   WHAT YOU NEED TO DRAW YOUR DAY   11

PART THREE   HOW TO DRAW YOUR DAY   23

PART FOUR   WHAT TO DRAW   59

PART FIVE   PUTTING IT ALL TOGETHER   111

PART SIX   A VISIT TO MY STUDIO   131

START YOUR JOURNAL HERE   136

PART ONE
WHY DRAW YOUR DAY?

YOU ARE AN ARTIST

Do you keep a diary? Do you like to draw? Are you not sure if you like to draw but want to try? When we think of a journal, we usually think of just writing, but this book is all about keeping a visual journal filled with drawings that you create to show the things you do, see, and eat during your days. Drawing your daily life helps you learn so much about yourself and the world around you. From the biggest events, like getting braces, to the smallest stuff, like tasting a new food for the first time, tracking it all in one place is so much fun. And I'm excited to tell you how to do it.

We all start to draw, in our own unique way, from the time we can hold a crayon in our hands. It's only later, when we begin to compare our drawing to others, that we sometimes get discouraged and lose the confidence to continue. But I want you to know that you *are* an artist, and you *can* draw! In this book, you will see many drawings that look just like what I intended—an ice pop that looks like an ice pop, a dog that looks like a dog. But what you don't see is all the patience and practice it took for me to be able to draw like I do!

Keep an open mind! The great thing about drawing is that there are a million ways to do it—it is ART, after all, and art comes in so many different forms. Through regular practice, you will get better and find your own unique style. I promise! And if you draw the things you do each day, the things you eat, the things you see, and the places you go, then you will never run out of ideas and you will keep improving.

Creating an illustrated journal is a practice you can continue your whole life, from age eight to eighty! Imagine looking back at this journal in twenty years. How cool will that be? There may be times you stop for a while, but it will always be there for you to start up again. You may enjoy drawing your days more on a special trip, or to remember a difficult time or a really exciting time. Or, like me, you may enjoy doing this each and every day. Some months you may pick it up often, some months not at all. Whenever and however you choose is perfectly fine. Let this be the beginning of a lifelong ritual!

"CREATIVITY TAKES COURAGE." —HENRI MATISSE

A NEW GLUE GUN

PUBLIC ENTRANCE 1

A TRIP TO BR WITH KERI, THEN APRIL ⟹ a triple coffee date! Then F to 14th Street to BARNEY's store for beauty bag and lunch on the way. HOME FOR PICKUP, and A WORK & SKETCHBOOK SESSION FROM 2:45-5:45. COOKING @ 6:30 PM — Taco dinner.

T's FIRST DAY of 3rd grade! We walk to school @ 8 am and its a reunion for all the kids and parents. It takes us an hour to leave school.

september 8th, 2016

SUN & HEAT high 87° in NYC

A FEW THINGS TO KEEP IN MIND:

- Like me, you might find that drawing is easier than writing out your thoughts and feelings. Keep your mind open to all the possibilities!

- Did you know that learning to write the letters of the alphabet is a form of drawing? So you're already drawing and you didn't even know it!

- Anyone can draw. Yes, that means you! It's how you choose to draw that becomes your unique style. It doesn't have to be perfect. In fact, some very famous artists intentionally draw things in a very imperfect way! Have you ever seen Picasso's paintings?

- Drawing and painting are fun! Remember that the more you draw, the better, so try not to be too critical of what you create. Eventually you will create drawings and paintings that you love. It is well worth the practice to get there.

Let's get started!

HOW TO USE THIS BOOK:

- There will be lots of drawing exercises! Some may require testing your materials and making rough sketches and scribbles, so it is a good idea to have some extra paper on hand.
- The beginning of the book is filled with ideas, lessons, and prompts that you can complete over time or whenever you would like some inspiration.
- At the end of the book, you will find pages to fill with your own drawing and adventures when you're ready to start your journal.

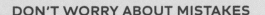

DON'T WORRY ABOUT MISTAKES

Remember that it is okay to make mistakes. In fact, mistakes can be fun! A mistake can turn into something new—an unplanned mark can become a pattern if you suddenly make more of them, or you can transform an ink blob into an ant crawling around your page. Drawing your days is as much about getting better at making art as it is about capturing and recording your memories. It is very gratifying to look back and see how much you have improved over time.

This book is meant to be a keepsake for years to come. My hope is that you fill it with all the amazing things that make up your current days so that you can remember them in the future.

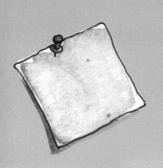

PART TWO
WHAT YOU NEED TO DRAW YOUR DAY

TOOLS AND MATERIALS

There are some art supplies that are helpful when drawing your days, but really anything you already own will work. You don't have to spend a lot of money on tools. From your school pencils to crayons to colored pencils, just grab what you have and get started! It is not about the tools you use but about regular practice.

If you find you love drawing, then you can collect more supplies over time.

Some amazing sketchbook artists use just a pencil or a ballpoint pen!

PENCILS

Use pencils to lightly sketch your drawings and to plan your pages. I find pencils to be the most useful tool because you can erase!

The graphite in the center of your pencil (the part that makes the marks on your paper) can be really soft (like a crayon) or really hard and firm. The graphite goes by a grading system from 9H (H for "hard") to 9B (B for "black"). The harder the graphite, the lighter the marks it will make. And the blacker the graphite, the darker the marks it will make. Right in the middle is the familiar Number 2 school pencil that you use all the time. Sometimes you will see "HB" on your pencil, which stands for "hard black" or medium hardness. My favorite pencils to use are a 2B or 3B. I like a slightly softer pencil because I can make really dark marks by pushing hard, and also keep my lines super light if I barely touch the point to the paper. Choosing a drawing pencil is personal, though, and it's fun to experiment to find what you like best.

ERASERS

The eraser on the back of a pencil isn't the best for drawing. I recommend you use a separate, big eraser. This way you can erase more marks at once! After trying out a bunch, I have found that plastic erasers work best. They are gentler on your paper and really pull off all the marks. Erasers will usually say "plastic" on the packaging, and they are often white in color.

PENS

After I sketch in pencil, I like to go over my drawings with a fine-line pen. I like the way it looks and find it's easier to color my drawings with a clear black outline. It's best to use pens with waterproof ink so that if you decide to paint or use water-soluble pencils or pastels (see page 16), the ink will not run. I recommend starting with a few Pigma Micron pens. They're very easy to find, come in a few thicknesses, and are inexpensive. Once you find the thickness you like best, you can buy more. Faber-Castell Pitt pens or Copic Multiliners are also great options.

Even if you decide to color or paint your drawings without ink, having these pens will be useful for the writing portion of your journal. On page 121, we will talk about typography and lettering, and adding captions and notes to go with your art. Having a permanent fine-line pen or two will be helpful for these purposes.

COLORED PENCILS AND WATER-SOLUBLE COLORED PENCILS

There are a lot of colored pencil options to choose from. If you have a school set, that will do just fine! If you would like more colors, there are some really great sets that have twelve colors to over a hundred colors (hello, holiday or birthday present)!

Some colored pencils are water soluble, meaning you can add water to make their colors spread over your page like watercolor paint. They are great to experiment with because you can color your drawings just like you would with regular colored pencils, and then decide later if you want to add some water. It is fun to have the option.

CRAYONS, PASTELS, AND WATER-SOLUBLE PASTELS

There are many different types of crayons or pastels. Some make marks like chalk and are not ideal for your journal because they get your fingers messy and the colors rub off on the opposite page. Others are smooth like your school crayons. I love water-soluble pastels the most! They work the same way as the water-soluble pencils do, but the pigment goes down really smoothly and in thicker lines. Then you can add water and see all the magic happen!

WATERCOLOR MARKERS AND PENS

There are markers that actually have watercolor paint right inside the barrel (the long part that you hold). You can squeeze to let a little or a lot out as you work. These are a ton of fun to use! But be careful not to squeeze too much paint at once. You can use your scrap paper to test just how much to squeeze or push before you commit on your final drawings.

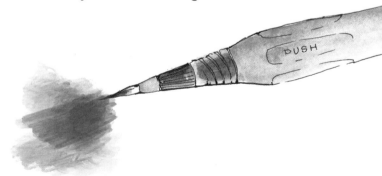

WATERCOLOR PALETTES

Paint palettes are so much fun to shop for
because there are so many to choose from!
But remember, from the paints you have at school
to the ones that artists use, you can create amazing art
with any of them. I started with an inexpensive set of paints
and stuck with it for years. I liked it because the colors were
vibrant, and it came with a waterbrush (explained more in the
brush section). It was also small, so I could throw it in my bag
and use it to paint outside or in a café.

There are student-grade and artist-grade watercolors. I suggest
you start with the student grade and work your way up.

BRUSHES

If you really like to paint, you'll want to get a few brushes for different purposes. Brushes differ in size, shape, and bristle type. You'll want various sizes to paint small and large areas, and all the in-betweens. Different-shaped brushes allow you to paint a variety of lines and shapes, from straight and flat areas to round and flowing lines. You can get brushes that are made of plastic, or you can get brushes made with real hair (horse hair!) that you can keep for a long time. Waterbrushes hold water in the barrel, which you squeeze out a little bit at a time to activate the paints in your palette. You can also use waterbrushes with water-soluble markers, pencils, and crayons.

OTHER TOOLS

It is nice to have a glue stick and a small pair of scissors around when you draw your days. This way, if you have a candy wrapper, a ticket stub, or some other small memento, you can glue it down and paint and draw around it (more on this on pages 88–89).

A small pencil sharpener is also helpful. I like to sketch with a sharp pencil!

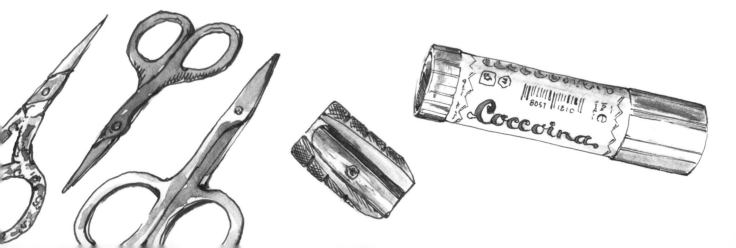

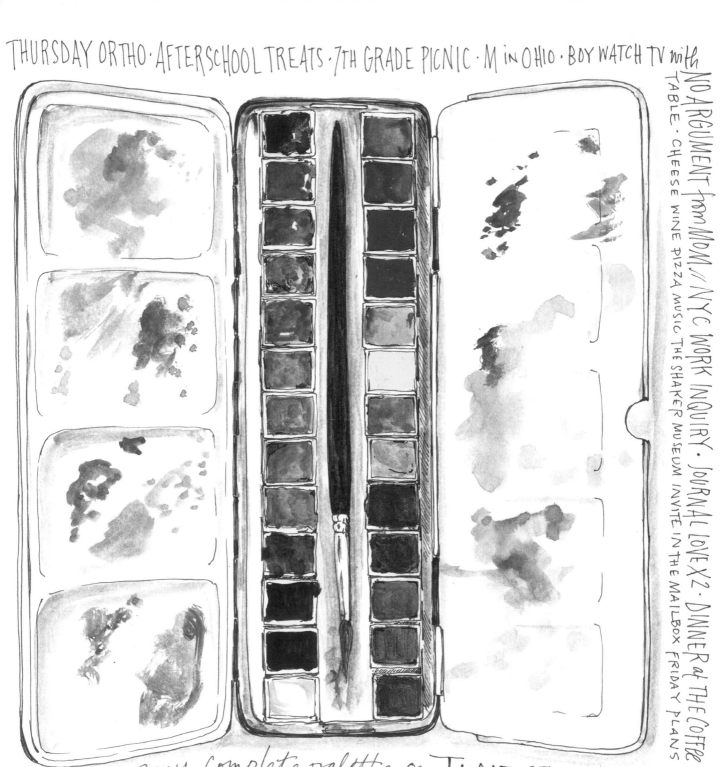

THURSDAY ORTHO · AFTERSCHOOL TREATS · 7TH GRADE PICNIC · M in OHIO · BOY WATCH TV with NO ARGUMENT from MOM // NYC WORK INQUIRY · JOURNAL LOVE X2 · DINNER at THE COFFEE TABLE · CHEESE WINE PIZZA MUSIC THE SHAKER MUSEUM INVITE IN THE MAILBOX FRIDAY PLANS

my complete palette on JUNE 15, 2017

CREATING YOUR ARTIST'S TOOL KIT

Now that you have gathered all the tools you need to begin drawing your days, I recommend that you keep them in one tote bag or box in your room. (An empty shoebox is a great option!) This way you can bring your art supplies with you to draw your days wherever you choose. Some days you might want to set up on the kitchen table; other days you might want to sketch in a special corner of your room. You can even bring your supplies in the car for a family road trip.

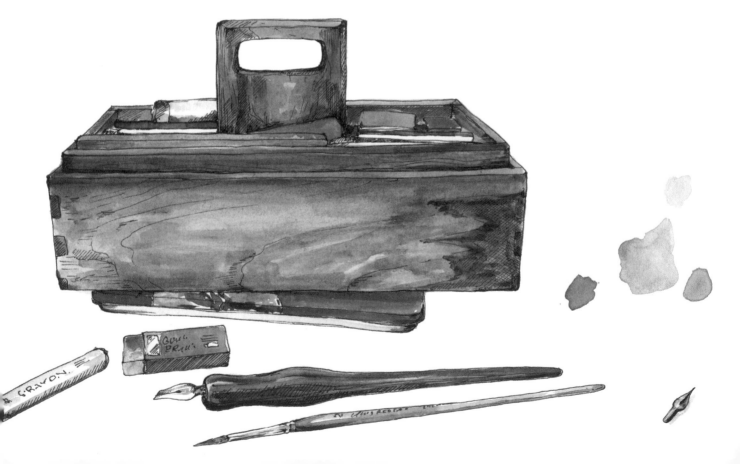

I bring my journal with me everywhere I go so that whenever I feel inspired, my pencil and sketchbook are always within reach. I will draw anywhere—in line at the grocery store, on a park bench, waiting for my food to arrive at a restaurant. If you create a smaller travel-sized art kit, you can draw anywhere too! I keep an easy-to-carry plastic pouch packed with essential tools so I can grab it whenever I leave home. Ask your mom or dad for a big gallon-sized plastic storage bag or some type of plastic pouch and stock it with a pencil, a big eraser, and maybe a small watercolor palette or some markers. Then just add your sketchbook, and you're all set!

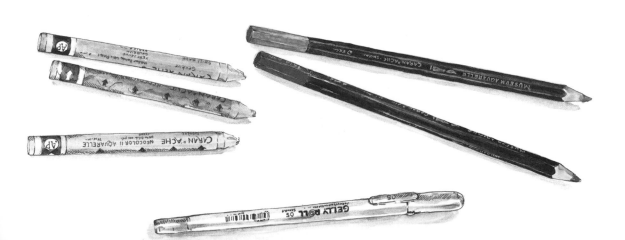

PART THREE
HOW TO DRAW YOUR DAY

COVER WORK DRAWINGS of AN OLD BARN and PATTERN BOR- DERS another night discussing HOMEWORK A FRESH DIRECT order with ALMONDS and GRAPEFRUIT A SHARED SAND- WICH and TONS OF PEN & PENCIL SORTING

11·6·17

THERE ARE SO MANY WAYS TO DRAW!

When I say "how to draw," I mean that we will try some basic exercises and tricks that can help you work on your drawings so that they can be as exact as you wish them to be.

Sometimes your drawings will take on a life of their own. You will have an idea in your head, but when you put pen to paper, your marks wind up creating a drawing that looks very different from what you planned. In order to get your artwork closer to what you picture, you have to practice, and knowing some basic rules about drawing techniques can help you reach your goals. Always know that along the way, however your drawings appear on paper, they are uniquely yours and are wonderful! Even the greatest artists in the world had to learn some rules before they determined their own personal style. You might surprise yourself by discovering that something you think is imperfect is actually quite perfect!

There is no wrong way to draw or make art.

GETTING READY TO DRAW

Let's begin with a few simple drawing exercises. These are meant to be loose and free. You can use the areas provided to practice them, but I also recommend having extra scrap paper nearby so that you can fill as many pages as you are inspired to fill. Have your supplies ready to go, and remember to have fun!

MAKING MARKS

Before you begin to dive into your actual drawings, it is a good idea to get comfortable with the tools you will be using. When you buy a new pencil or a new set of water-soluble pastels, get a few scrap pieces of paper and simply make some marks. What happens if you push really hard? What happens if you push softly, barely touching the point of your pen or pencil to the page?

lightest touch to the darkest

Art supplies can do so many things to make your work more special, but sometimes they can be unpredictable. The colors may look different on paper than they do on the packaging. Or the lines that a pen or pastel makes can be thicker or thinner than you expected. Getting familiar with what your tools can and cannot do will help you to plan your finished art a little better.

USE THIS PAGE TO MAKE LINES AND CIRCLES, OR BIG SCRIBBLES WITH YOUR TOOLS.

"WE DON'T MAKE MISTAKES, JUST HAPPY LITTLE ACCIDENTS." -BOB ROSS

Sometimes drips of ink
or paint can be a fun
addition to your artwork,
but if unplanned, they can
be upsetting!

PENCIL OR COLORED PENCIL FROM LIGHT TO DARK

Now that you have played around making some loose lines and marks, let's see how different tools can create lines from light to dark, depending on how you use them. When you press harder, the pencil will create darker marks. When you keep your hand loose and barely press down at all, the lines you create will be very light. Experiment with pressure to learn to create the shades of tone you want.

USE ONE TOOL TO FILL THE BOXES IN FIVE DIFFERENT SHADES. Fill each of the squares below using the same pencil or colored pencil of your choice. Start with the lightest pressure, then gradually add more pressure (pushing a little bit harder with your point) as you fill each box. The first box should be the lightest shade, and the last box should be the darkest!

You can do this exercise with as many pencils as you choose on scrap paper to see how each one performs differently going from lightest to darkest. You can also do this with paint by varying the amount of water to make the color less and more intense.

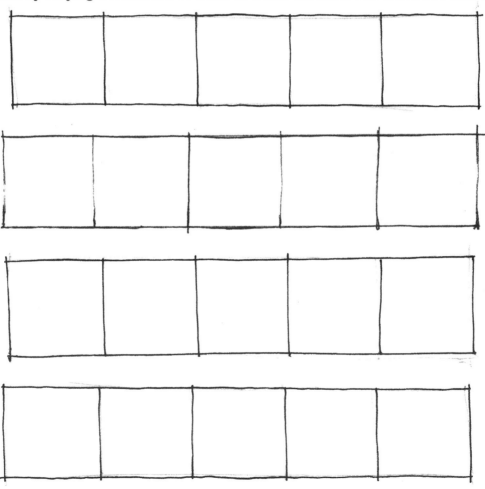

HOW TO "SEE"

Now it is almost time to begin to draw. But before we do, I want to talk about seeing. Seeing is a really, really important first step to begin any drawing practice. Any subject that you attempt to draw on paper will begin to look different to you once you really look at it with the intention of drawing it. For example, let's take a simple pencil. We know that a pencil is round or hexagonal, we know that it has some words or numbers on one side, we know it usually has an eraser held at the top with a piece of metal, called a *ferrule*, and so on. But if we were to draw the pencil, we'd start to notice so many more details.

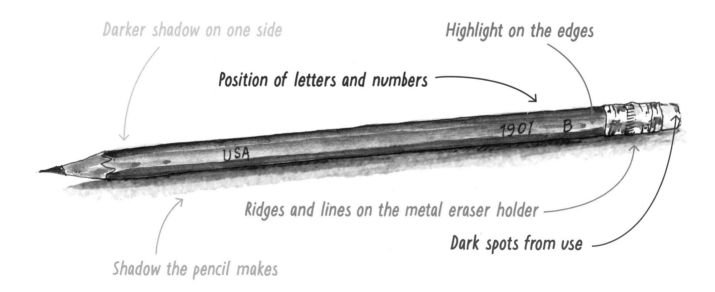

Darker shadow on one side

Highlight on the edges

Position of letters and numbers

Ridges and lines on the metal eraser holder

Dark spots from use

Shadow the pencil makes

So before you begin to create your artwork, look at your subject long enough to see the shapes and sizes of all the different parts. If you draw a new pair of jeans, you have to look at the length of the legs or how the pockets are shaped. If you draw your lunch, imagine being a tiny ant crawling around the edge of your plate and note what the food looks like. Or focus on the space around your subject (also known as *negative space*). We will talk more about this on page 118.

TIP: *Take some time looking. Really pause before you dive in. It will pay off, trust me!*

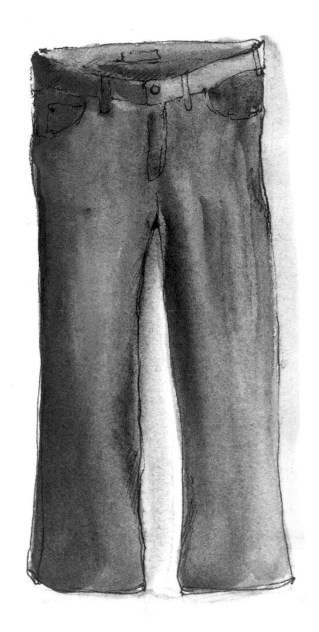

DRAWING LIGHT AND SHADOW

If you would like your subject to come to life and pop off your page, it is important to learn about light and shading. Similar to perspective, this is a complex subject that can be studied in depth, but I am going to give you a basic overview. A piece of fruit is a great place to start, as it is typically very familiar. It is usually round, so the shadows curve nicely around it, making it a perfect subject to practice light and shading. Place your fruit on a white surface so that the shadows underneath are easy to see as you begin to study and experiment. As illustrated in the example here, you will see that the main light source is coming from the top right. Note that where the light hits your fruit is going to be the lightest point, or the highlight. As the apple curves away from the light, your shading will get progressively darker until it is in complete darkness on the opposite side. The shadow will also fall away from the light. So if the light is coming from the upper right, the shadow will be to the left. A great way to see where the darkest and lightest areas are is to squint your eyes. Even when the subject is full of vibrant color, such as a red apple, squinting your eyes helps to focus on the darkest and lightest places to translate onto your paper.

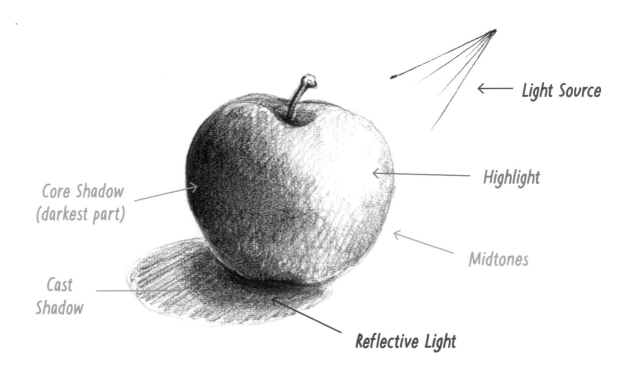

Light Source

Highlight

Core Shadow (darkest part)

Midtones

Cast Shadow

Reflective Light

BLIND CONTOUR DRAWING

As you look and think about everything you see, from the big picture to the littlest details, one of the best drawing warm-up exercises is to draw your subject without looking at your paper. This exercise is called *blind contour*. *Blind* meaning you don't look at what you are creating, so it is almost as if you are blindfolded. And *contour* meaning that you are drawing only outlines and edges, without any shading. Do this without stopping and making changes, even if you're tempted to "fix" your drawing along the way. And don't look down at your paper! If it sounds like these drawings will be really silly looking, they will be! That's part of the fun, and the whole point of doing them. Even the most talented artists will make very funny-looking blind contour drawings. The results can open you up to a new way of thinking about art and change your ideas about what is perfect and what is possible.

Blind contour really helps you to see better and draw better. These drawings take just a minute or so, and I recommend drawing them without lifting your pen or pencil off the page! Try drawing a bottle like I did here.

TIP: *Try really hard not to look while you're drawing! The less you look down at your paper, the more carefree your drawings will be. And when you are finished and do look down, you will discover a fun surprise! It might even make you laugh. And better yet, you might love what you create.*

CREATE A FEW OF YOUR OWN BLIND CONTOUR DRAWINGS.

TIP: *Place your paper to your side, rather than right in front of you. This way, as you are creating your drawing, it will be harder to look over at it because you will have to turn your head toward your paper.*

FROM SKETCH TO COLOR

BEGIN WITH A PENCIL SKETCH

I like to use a sharp pencil to start all my journal pages. I sketch out my plan for each page and figure out where things will go.

Your sketches can be as detailed as you wish. Some people make a very light, loose sketch in pencil, and then begin adding pen, paint, or marker. Others like to create a more detailed pencil drawing before finishing in color or pen. The advantage of a light, loose sketch is that you can very easily erase all your marks and move or change your art. On the other hand, an elaborate or detailed sketch that you spend more time on can bring you closer to your final art. Pencil sketches can be

beautiful, so keep in mind that your final art can be just your pencil drawing if you choose. I recommend you play around and practice to see what kind of sketch process works for you.

Sketching with a light touch takes patience and practice. You may tend to press down as hard as you do in school to write on your assignments, but drawing with a pencil is different from writing. Sometimes you will make lots of marks to create a shape until you are happy with your work. Then you can press harder to make it darker. I like to see all the light and dark marks in my sketches, and I actually don't erase all my marks. I believe there is beauty in the layers.

Whether you erase your pencil marks or not is up to you! But if you choose to erase your pencil and you have used colored pencil on top, erasing at the end may take off some of the color. Or if you use paint, erasing later may smudge the colors. Experiment so that you know what to expect and how to plan.

TIP: *Remember to have a light touch at first, and then add more pressure as you work. If you press too hard, you will make grooves in your paper that you will not be able to erase with your eraser.*

41

Sketch lightly and start with the overall shape before adding the small
details. As you can see in my example, I started by drawing a very light
outline of my friend's dog. Then, once I was happy with the overall
shape and size, I began to add more details.

SKETCH SOMETHING SIMPLE. Find a simple subject like a flower or a piece of fruit and sketch it very lightly in pencil with lots of loose, free lines. Draw it a few times so you can practice building layers. As you feel confident about where your lines are, you can add pressure to make the lines darker and your drawing more finished.

FROM PENCIL TO INK

Once the pencil is finished, it is completely up to you how you will take your drawings to the next level! There are so many possibilities, but I like to outline my pencil sketches in ink and add detail with my pen before I add paint. I also love to leave some of my ink drawings alone and not add color at all, because I am so pleased with how they look. My favorite pens to use are fully waterproof and have a fine tip. A black Pigma Micron 01 or 02 is a great choice, but you can also experiment making ink drawings with any pen you have. Just keep in mind that some might bleed or smudge when you add other markers or wet paint on top of the ink if they are not labeled "waterproof."

There are a few shading techniques that you can use your pens to practice. My favorite is called *crosshatching*. Crosshatching happens when you make a series of parallel lines (lines that go in the same direction) along the edges of your shapes to create shadows and depth. The more overlapping lines you make, the darker the area becomes. Another technique is called *stippling*. Stippling happens when you make a series of dots to create depth and shadow. The more dots, and the closer together they are, the darker an area becomes.

PENCIL SKETCH

FIRST INK: OUTLINE, ADDING WEIGHT FOR A SUGGESTION OF DIMENSION AND SHADOW.

CROSSHATCHING: A SERIES OF OVERLAPPING LINES.

STIPPLING: A SERIES OF DOTS.

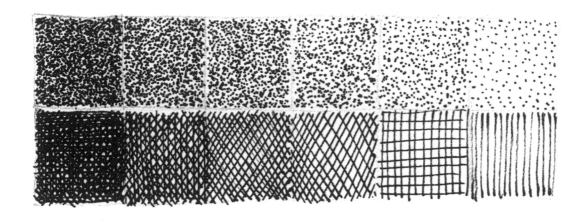

SHADING IN INK

IN THE SPACE BELOW, PRACTICE CROSSHATCHING AND STIPPLING. You can fill the empty boxes with more and more lines for crosshatching, and more and more dots for stippling, going from light to dark.

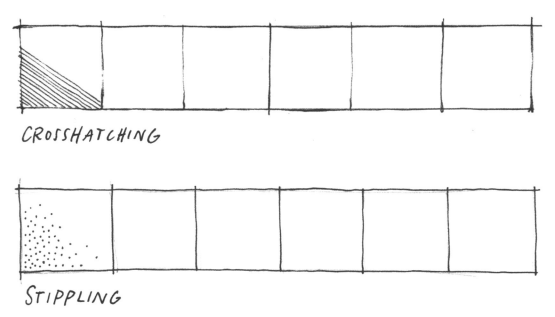

CROSSHATCHING

STIPPLING

LEARNING ABOUT COLOR

COLORS CAPTURE FEELINGS

When you think of color, the first thing that may come to mind is the rainbow. The colors red, orange, yellow, green, blue, and purple appear after the rain, and these stripes represent a happy new beginning when the sun starts to shine.

You see, color can make us feel things and so can combinations of color. Have you ever seen a piece of food that isn't the most pleasing color and you decide that you don't want to try it? Or have you seen a flower in a garden that is the brightest pink, and it makes your eyes open wider because it is so beautiful?

a happy colorful little bird in the park

PRIMARY COLORS

SECONDARY COLORS

RED AND BLUE MAKE
PURPLE

YELLOW AND RED MAKE
ORANGE

BLUE AND YELLOW
MAKE GREEN

PRIMARY AND SECONDARY COLORS

In your artwork, you get to choose the colors you use. Some of your paint sets or pastels might have only a few colors, but as long as you have just three basic colors, you can create an endless amount of other colors just by mixing them. These three colors are called *primary colors,* and they are red, yellow, and blue. When you mix these three together, you get more colors, known as *secondary colors.* Yellow and blue make green, red and yellow make orange, and blue and red make purple. And now you have the rainbow! But it doesn't stop there. You can mix all these primary and secondary colors together to get more and more colors, even hundreds!

What I find just as important as creating or finding the exact color of what I am drawing are the combinations I choose across my whole page. Color can create a feeling, color can make us remember a time, and color can create a pleasing composition across your page. (See more about composition on page 114.)

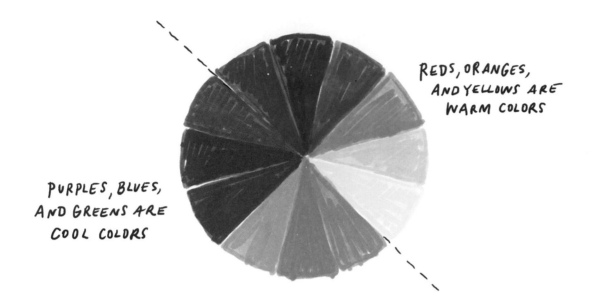

REDS, ORANGES, AND YELLOWS ARE WARM COLORS

PURPLES, BLUES, AND GREENS ARE COOL COLORS

WARM AND COOL COLORS

Let's talk a little more about the feelings that color can create. In the science of color—yep, there is a whole science behind color—reds, oranges, and yellows are considered *warm colors,* and they are known to represent a more excited feeling. They also can represent warmth like a fire, or anger or frustration or embarrassment. (Think of our cheeks getting pink when we blush.) Blues, greens, and purples are known as *cool colors,* and they represent icy coldness and sometimes sadness, while also expressing comfort and calm. Have you ever heard someone say they feel "blue," meaning sad? Although there are associations made about color that we can learn, I believe that they are not always true. I love all blues, and my favorite color is green—these colors make me feel happy because I just like them. Liking a color is enough to use it in your art!

CHOOSING COLORS

Knowing a bit about how colors work when mixed together is really important for any artist, and deciding what colors you would like to use can feel overwhelming, especially if you have lots of options right in front of you. I suggest that you keep it simple. Choose art supplies that come in sets of fifteen to thirty colors. You will be able to do so much with that amount of color options. I find that if my paint selection (also known as *paint palette*) is too large, I get overwhelmed. I tend to keep mine to about twenty colors, and then I can mix others as needed.

TIP: *Just know that you have the freedom to use any colors you like. A tree does not have to be green if you would rather use blue. And a banana can be purple if you want it to be!*

49

ADDING COLOR

Whether you choose markers, colored pencils, paints, pastels, crayons, or a mix of a few of these tools, adding color to your artwork is the finishing touch and is so much fun. I suggest keeping it simple at first. You can color parts of your drawing as you would in a coloring book, using solid colors to fill an area without adding light and dark tones. Or you could add shading, meaning that one side is a bit darker to indicate shadow or lighter to show a highlighted area.

Continue to try new techniques on scrap paper so you can decide what you like best. Once you pick your favorite, keep practicing it on your scrap paper before making your final drawings in your journal. Eventually, you won't need to go through so many different steps and practice versions. But at the beginning, it's a learning process.

A highlight is the area of your subject that is the lightest or whitest. It indicates the part that the light hits.

COLOR EACH SKETCH ON THE RIGHT BY USING THE SAME COLORING TECHNIQUE AND ART MEDIUM I'VE DEMONSTRATED ON THE LEFT.

Use colored pencils to create flat, solid colors.

Use water-soluble pastels or colored pencils. Add darker areas for shading, and keep an area white for highlights.

Use watercolor paints. Add darker areas for shading, and keep an area white for highlights.

SHADING A BALL

Find something round to draw, like a ball, an apple, or a few grapes. First, place your subject in front of you and just simply look at the darkest and lightest parts. Do you see the highlight (the whitest part where the light is hitting the side of the fruit)? Do you see the shadows (the darkest part farthest from the light)?

NEXT BEGIN TO SKETCH YOUR ROUND OBJECT IN PENCIL. Start with a regular pencil, very lightly at first, because it's the easiest to erase. Once you like the shape of this outline sketch, begin to fill it with color. Leave a little part of the paper white where the highlight is. Add more intense or darker color where the shadows are. You can do this by layering a darker color on top of a lighter one, or by adding more pressure to make the color darker like we did earlier in our boxes.

DRAW THE SAME SUBJECT THREE WAYS

It is really fun to explore drawing one subject in many different styles. As you can see from my example, I captured some flowers three different ways. The first flowers are very loose and free, painted with flat, solid color, almost as if they are cartoons of flowers. The second is painted loosely without an ink outline. The lines are free flowing, making the flower look a little more abstract (meaning it doesn't look *exactly* like a flower, but you can still tell it is one). The last flower is a very realistic drawing using ink and watercolor.

IN THE SPACE BELOW, TRY DRAWING A FLOWER IN THREE DIFFERENT STYLES. Use various art supplies to make each flower unique.

LIFE

DRAW FROM LIFE, MEMORY, AND A PHOTOGRAPH

One of my favorite drawing experiments is to draw the same subject from real life—as I see it in front of me—then from a photograph for reference (I take a picture on my phone and look at the photo as I draw), and finally a third time just from memory. I want you to try this too! It is a wonderful way to get to know what you are drawing. And very often I find that I like the version drawn from memory the best. Give it a try and see what you prefer. Use three different pieces of scrap paper for this exercise.

1.   Find something to draw, like a plant or a favorite toy or a vase filled with flowers. Sit down with your

paper and pencils or pens, and look at your subject as you draw. Start with the overall shape before adding the smaller parts. Spend a little time with this drawing.

2. Take a photo of the same subject you just drew—you might need to ask an adult to help you. Make sure you take the photo from the same angle to show your subject looking the same as it did when you drew it from life.

    Now draw it again by looking at the photograph. Often we will think of things we want to draw, but we don't know exactly what they look like. Using a photo to show you the details while you work is very common for an artist.

3. Now that you've drawn the same thing twice, you are pretty familiar with it. You remember the details and the basic shapes. Try drawing it again using only your memory.

    When you are finished, look at all three drawings and think about which process you enjoyed the most. Which finished version do you like the best? Which one makes you feel the most proud?

MEMORY
←

PHOTO
↘

PART FOUR
WHAT TO DRAW

INSPIRATION FOR DRAWING YOUR DAY

I know that a blank page can feel a little intimidating or scary. I have stared at a new blank page thousands of times! Sometimes I know exactly what I will draw, but often I do not, and I have to give it a bit of time and thought. How I get past this uncertainty is to simply think about all that I did that day. What did I eat? Did I get some exercise? Did I pass by someone or something interesting in the park? What is the weather like outside my window? You see, if you think about your days, even the little things we do like combing our hair or having breakfast, then the possibilities of what to draw are endless! In fact, sometimes it is as simple as looking right in front of you! What are some of your favorite things in your room? What do you have on your desk or hanging on the walls above where you are sitting?

DRAW ONE THING YOU SEE RIGHT NOW. Look around you at this very moment. Look to your left, to your right, below your table, up at the ceiling, on the walls, or outside your window, and pick one thing to draw.

DAILY RITUALS

Now let's dig a little deeper into our days to find inspiration. Think about all your daily rituals or habits. What are some of the very first things you do each morning? I am sure you brush your teeth; then you might have some breakfast, or maybe you pet your cat or dog? How do you choose what you will wear each day? Do you lay your outfit out the night before? Do you take any vitamins or medicine? Do you practice playing a musical instrument each day?

   Now think about all the different ways that you can draw these daily rituals. Let's take brushing your teeth. You can simply draw a toothbrush with some toothpaste; that would be perfectly fine. But there are many other creative ways to capture brushing your teeth on paper. Maybe you draw a very close-up detail of the bristles and toothpaste sitting on top. Or maybe you draw a bunch of blue scribbles and circles to represent the foamy, sudsy toothpaste as you scrub your teeth.

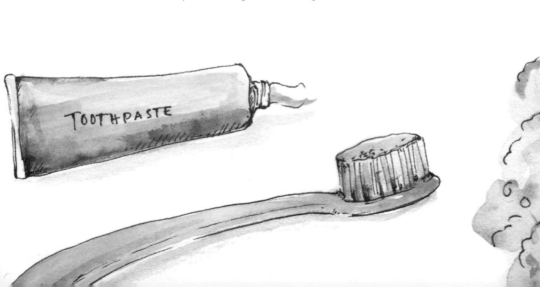

DRAW A RITUAL THREE WAYS. If you're drawing a musical practice, think about the music notes you read as you play or think about drawing some fluid, loose lines moving around your page to symbolize the sounds in the music. You might also simply draw your instrument. If you play a sport, draw your uniform, the gear you use, or the green grass you play on. If you dance, draw your dance shoes or the ballet barre at the dance studio.

DRAW YOUR MOOD

Another way to tackle the blank page is to think about how you are feeling. Sometimes how and what we choose to draw is determined by our mood. Some days you will want to practice drawing things just as they are, and other days you might want to draw lots of marks and lines and abstract patterns instead. The benefit of drawing your day in any way you choose is that each time you sit down to create, you will wind up with a completely different expression and finished artwork. We don't feel the same every day, so our pages should not look the same every day.

Some days I make abstract art, and other days I focus really hard drawing one thing exactly as I see it. When you are faced with a challenge like drawing your friend or your pet, sometimes it can be a really icky feeling because the drawing doesn't turn out just like you wanted it to. I know when a subject will be more difficult for me, I really need to be up for the challenge, and some days I am just not in the mood. On the days when I feel a little more sensitive or tired, I will draw something easier or I will fill a page with color and writing. Remember that drawing colors and patterns is also a way to draw your day!

Abstract art uses lines, forms, shapes, and color to represent your message or feeling.

HAPPY DAY   SLOW, BORING DAY   STRESSFUL DAY

YOUR MOOD IN COLOR

What color do you feel today? Do you feel bright orange and
yellow because you are excited and happy? Or do you feel a
little blue because the weather is gloomy and you can't play
outside? Or do you feel green because you had to eat some
green vegetables for dinner?

Anything from abstract patterns to realistic drawings can
represent how you feel. You can even draw something in an
unusual color, like a bright, happy orange test paper because
you got a good grade.

DRAWING CHALLENGE

FILL EACH MOOD BOX WITH A PICTURE OR PATTERN THAT SHOWS DIFFERENT FEELINGS.
You can draw abstract patterns or something more realistic but try to use only one color for each box. Maybe you're happy because you are going on a trip. Draw your backpack in a bright, cheerful color. Or maybe you're down because it's too rainy to play outside. Draw what is outside your window in whatever color shows those feelings. You can even add a caption to remind your future self why you made your backpack orange or the wet tree outside blue.

3·27·19

a butterfly in the park
Pepper opening the door
RAIN ALL DAY

Even on a gray, rainy day, you can lift your spirits by drawing
a colorful butterfly or a friendly animal.

MORE THINGS YOU CAN DRAW

WEATHER

The weather can have a pretty big effect on our days. A long, hot sunny day can be tiring and sweaty. A freezing cold day can make our toes feel numb. A rainy day can cancel our plans . . . or lead to a cozy day inside . . . or can also be, well, wet! I have found over the years that the weather is one of the most fun things to draw on a journal page. You can make patterns of raindrops to fill extra spaces, you can add a bright yellow sun to the background or in the corner of your page, or you can make a mountain of snow along the bottom of your page. The weather can inspire drawing things like sleds, snowmen, mittens, hats and scarves, umbrellas, rain boots, yellow rain ponchos, bathing suits, swimming goggles, a pool float, sun hats, a handheld fan to cool you off, and so much more! I hope you will feel inspired to draw the weather after you fill the following pages with some of your creative ideas.

AT 6:45 PM LAST NIGHT, WE ARE NOTIFIED THAT NYC SCHOOLS WILL BE CLOSED 2DAY We sleep in until 9am and it feels like an extension of holiday break T PLAY MINECRAFT WITH LUKE all MORNING WHILE IAN DOES WORK & FIGHTS A COLD. M WORKS at THE DINING ROOM TABLE. I WORK at Kitchen Counter while standing

SNOW DAY

BOMB CYCLONE STORM OUTSIDE · COZY SLIPPERS AND TEA INSIDE ·

Jan 4th 2018

DRAW THE WEATHER WRITTEN ABOVE EACH BOX.

A hot and muggy day

A very windy and crisp fall day

A snowstorm or blizzard

A wet and rainy day

DRAW THE WEATHER IN YOUR OWN UNIQUE WAY. Look outside and think about how you can draw the weather. How is it making you feel? Be as expressive or straightforward as you like. You can just draw a sun or raindrops, or you can draw a whole scene.

NATURE

Whether you live in the city or the country or somewhere in between, you are surrounded by nature! Just look up at the sky . . . at the trees on your street . . . or at yourself in the mirror. (Yes, you are part of the natural world!) If you live outside the city, then I am sure all you have to do is look out your window to see some green grass or a few trees. But if you live in a city, you can still find grass or leaves peeking out from under the sidewalk or around buildings. There are also urban parks lined with trees and window boxes filled with flowers. Nature is powerful and beautiful, and it exists wherever you live—you just have to look for it.

"there are no straight lines in nature."

~antoni gaudi

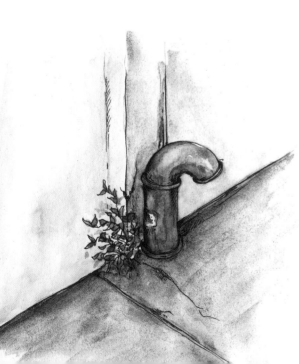

CENOTE
Snorkeling
Tacos in AKUMAL

LAST MINUTE ATM STOP for tips
and lunch

EL TACO MAYA WINDS UP BEING ONE OF OUR BEST MEALS for 24.00 (FOR ALL OF US)

2·2018

This bird
becomes a
bit of a pest
as we eat
nachos on
the
beach
→

PELICAN
SILOUETTE

Scene across the street from the Meyer family's
hotel in Tulum — on our last day we are all
a bit sad, and start talking about our next trip to
Mexico. Home to lots of chaos and a studio move!

Not only can you find inspiration by looking for nature around you, but I am pretty sure that you have drawn a flower or two already—plants, trees, flowers, birds, spiderwebs, insects are all easy to draw from your imagination and memory. If you saw a few ants crawling on your picnic blanket, you can try drawing them from memory, or you can look up photos of them to make your drawings more accurate. Flowers and leaves can fill empty spaces on your page, and since nature is always around, it is automatically a part of your days. So I encourage you to find fun ways to include bits and pieces of the natural world on your journal pages. Vines can make a border around your page or can fill little empty spaces in your composition. Leaves can be tall or short, wide or thin, and they can be any color of the rainbow. You can use the colors that you see in nature in other areas of your artwork too. For example, you can paint the date of your journal entry in the same green that you paint a tree that day.

DRAW NATURE THAT YOU SEE AROUND YOU. It's okay to either skip or replace one of these if you can't find something from your own home or outside.

Draw a tree you see through one of your windows at home.

Draw a pattern of leaves and flowers around the border.

Draw four leaves that you find outside, each in a different shape and color.

Draw a tiny insect, like an ant, a ladybug, or a spider, crawling on a flower.

ANIMALS

Do you have a pet? Or a favorite animal? One of my very favorite things to draw are animals because they bring me so much joy and they have so much character! From cats and dogs to insects and lizards to horses and giraffes, I will draw an animal any chance I get. I also find that I can be really playful with the features on an animal's face. Imperfections in an animal's face or body just give your drawings a personal flair.

You can draw an animal you've seen during the day. Or you can add fun to your journal page by having animals act out parts of your day through little drawings. Sometimes I will pretend that a dog I meet on the street is talking to me, and I make up the things they are saying. Maybe you create a recurring character in your journal that has a voice bubble above its head describing or narrating your thoughts. You can use images you find on the computer, photos on your phone, or drawings you made of your own pet or a friend's pet for practice. Eventually you can create the animals in your own personal style, and whether that is very realistic or cartoon-like, the animals you draw will be uniquely yours. Have fun experimenting with animal drawings!

MILOU ON THE SUBWAY IN A BAG

DRAW YOUR ANIMAL OF CHOICE AND WRITE ABOUT HOW THE ANIMAL MAKES YOU FEEL. Do you have a pet? Do you like petting the dogs you meet in your neighborhood? Does your friend have a cat? Even if you don't like interacting with animals in person, they are a lot of fun to draw!

DRAWING CHALLENGE

TRY DRAWING YOUR OWN PET OR A FRIEND'S PET WHILE IT'S ASLEEP. If you have a dog or a cat, you'll be familiar with their constant movement. Sometimes it is hard to even capture them in a photograph, let alone draw them! But animals all have to sleep, and I find that is the best time to practice drawing them because they are perfectly still.

8·8·17· Brooklyn Cat

A DEAD LEAF ON LAFAYETTE

EVERYDAY ACTIVITIES AND ITEMS

A lot of days can feel pretty repetitive and maybe a little boring. You have some breakfast, do your schoolwork, eat dinner, play some games, run around outside, read a book, go to sleep, and then do the same all over again. But if you think about the routine activities you do each day, like brushing your teeth (see page 63) or putting on your pajamas, then there is always something to draw. Some days may feel more interesting or exciting even though nothing extraordinary happened. Maybe you had a really good day at school, or you saw a movie with your family, or you went on a field trip. These activities can also be drawn in your journal alongside the simpler things. Everyday activities on an ordinary day will become more interesting when you focus and celebrate them on a journal page with your pencils, markers, and paints!

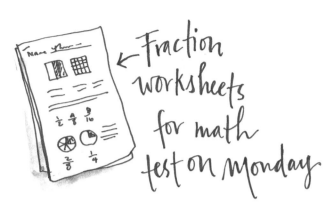

Fraction worksheets for math test on Monday

You can also draw the same things over and over because the more you draw something, the more your drawing skills will improve. Through regular practice, you will be able to draw something like your breakfast from memory. Also, the little things that make up your days will show your future self what you do and enjoy right now. Your favorite shoes today might not be your favorite a year from now. It is fun to look back!

A SNOWY, DRIPPY HAT HANGING FROM THE DOORKNOB

HERE ARE SOME ORDINARY THINGS THAT ARE REALLY FUN TO DRAW:

- YOUR DOG'S LEASH

- THE MILK CARTON FROM THE REFRIGERATOR

- YOUR FAVORITE SHOES

- A HAT HANGING BY THE DOOR

- THE VASE ON YOUR TABLE

- A VIDEO GAME CHARACTER

- A THEATER OR CONCERT TICKET

- A GLASS OF WATER

- YOUR FAVORITE SPORTS GEAR, BALL, OR JERSEY

- YOUR BOWL OF CEREAL

- YOUR HAT AND SCARF

- YOUR SCHOOLWORK OR BOOKS

WHAT ELSE CAN YOU THINK OF? WRITE A FEW MORE HERE:

_____   _____

_____   _____

_____   _____

_____   _____

_____   _____

_____   _____

walk
stella!

DRAW THREE THINGS THAT MAKE WHERE YOU LIVE FEEL LIKE HOME.

DRAW YOUR FAVORITE THINGS TO WEAR RIGHT NOW.

MAKE A LIST OF YOUR CHORES AND DRAW THEM IN A CREATIVE WAY.

A pumpkin-filled wagon
ON MAIN STREET, MANAYUNK, PA

SPECIAL EVENTS

Everything from competing in your school's field day to
going to see a Broadway show with your family is worth
celebrating and documenting in your journal. If the
Broadway show had really interesting costumes, you
can draw them! Or if you saw an animated movie with
fun characters, you can search for the characters online to
practice drawing them and also leave a little review of the
movie in your journal. If you won a game in the sport you
play, you can draw the winning score next to your
uniform or your team's logo. If you went to a

holiday dinner at your grandparents' house, you can draw some of the food you ate and write about the family members who were there with you. Getting a good grade on a test or making a new friend can also be considered special events! Whether big or small, what makes an event "special" is really up to you. And these special moments help you talk to your future self about how you felt and what you experienced.

MEMENTOS

A journal is the perfect place to store mementos from special events or any piece of paper that is meaningful, like a valentine, a note from a friend, a test you did well on, a ticket stub, or a theater program. You can glue these items down or draw a picture of them.

בזוקה
ללא סוכר
שוויאי / טייסה
ללא סוכר
בטעם בנוקה
28 גרם

STEADY
FLOW
OF
MINTS
and
GUM FOR
THEO

HIGH
105°
MASADA

רשות הטבע
והגנים
Israel Nature
and Parks Auth

No. 406576

NATIONAL PARK גן לאומי

מצדה
Masada
CABLE CAR - two ways ticket
רכבל מצדה – הלוך וחזור
ADULTS מבוגר

Masada
רכבל מצדה – הלוך וחזור
CABLE CAR - two ways ticket

YOUTH נוער

6 ADULT & 5 YOUTH
tram tickets

FLOATING IN
THE DEAD SEA

Early morning meet at bus to drive to Masada. It about 1.75 hr drive. When we get out, the heat is intense, but we are happy to feel a breeze in the shade, and the heat is without humidity, so bearable. We ride tram up, follow water bottles and learn a fair about King Herod. Bus to dead sea to swim. The water means are not to nice but we enjoy floating. Then to bedouin tents for dinner after camel rides led by an Australian playing Abraham.

july 2, 2018
MASADA | DEAD SEA | CAMEL RIDES
ERETZ BERESHEET + DINNER
UNDER A TENT ON OUR KNEES
WHICH IS A BIT TOURIST-Y, BUT STILL
INCREDIBLE, AND ONE OF OUR BEST MEALS
tonight we pack up for our Kibbutz in Galilee

FRIENDLY
STARLINGS
EAT FROM
OUR
HANDS

DRAWING CHALLENGE

DRAW A SPECIAL EVENT IN THE SPACE BELOW. Don't worry if you haven't done anything too exciting in the past week; you can also practice drawing an event that happened a few months ago, or an event that's coming up soon.

SLEEPOVERS

A sleepover at a friend's house is an escape from your normal life. There will be a new bed to sleep in, or a sleeping bag on the floor with your friend. You'll eat at a different dinner table and the food might be unfamiliar. You may love the new dishes and snacks, or miss the more familiar ones at home. You may watch movies, play games, or do crafts together. There could be a group of friends for a special night, or it might just be you and one friend.

Whatever the circumstances, a sleepover is absolutely something you will enjoy looking back on and remembering in the future.

TRAVEL—FROM SHORT TRIPS TO LONG VACATIONS

Travel is the most exciting time to draw your days. Trips, whether they are long or short, are filled with events that we want to remember.

Your family might spend weeks planning a big trip! Places you go might require a long drive, a train ride, or even an airplane adventure. Getting from one place to another can provide you with tons of drawing time (although it can be hard to draw in the car—I have tried many times!). And think about it: there is so much that is new to see, you can literally draw anything and everything!

When I travel, I always spend extra time thinking about what I will draw and write about in my journal. I don't want to forget anything. At the end of the day, when my family settles into our hotel room or the place we are staying, I look at all the photos I took and think about what was most interesting. Sometimes it's an obvious choice, like seeing a lizard in Mexico or taking a boat ride on the Long Island Sound. But other times it is a small moment that I don't want to forget, like looking up at an interesting building on the way to dinner. There is so much to think about and draw when you leave home and see the world from a new perspective. Bring this journal with you the next time you take a trip, and have fun drawing all the things you do, see, and eat along the way!

AUG·12 — DAY 3

A SPIDER ON THE WINDOW NEXT TO ME AT JON RIKI

A WHITE SHEEP WITH A SWEET BLACK NOSE AND BLACK EARS RIGHT OUTSIDE OF HOTEL AKUR

BLACK SAND BEACH

BLACK SAND BEACH ROCK COLLECTION → AFTER LUNCH IN VIK. IAN STAYS IN THE CAR TO REST MORE.

DRAW ALL THE THINGS YOU NEED TO PACK FOR A TRIP. Are you planning a trip anytime soon? Whether you visit a friend or grandparents for a weekend away or your family goes on vacation, you have to pack a bag, right? What are the most important things you need to take with you? Maybe your favorite blanket or pillow, or stuffed animal, and of course your toothbrush. What else do you need to bring along?

THINK ABOUT A TRIP YOU WENT ON AND DRAW A HIGHLIGHT HERE. Or better yet, take this journal with you on your next trip to do this in real time. What is your best memory? Was it something grand like climbing the Eiffel Tower in Paris, or was it a simple walk in a park? Even if it didn't happen today, our memories are very much a part of our days and worth drawing now.

THE CORNER of THE ROOM WE SLEEP IN ~ seen from the bed while watching TV with Ian

FAVORITE ROOMS IN YOUR HOME

We all have our very favorite places to settle in when we are home. Is there a specific table or desk that you like to sit at when you draw in this journal? Do you snuggle in a special spot on your couch when you watch TV? What about your bed or your bedroom? Is there a shelf that holds your favorite vacation souvenirs? Do you share your room with any siblings and divide the closet space or the drawers between you? Or maybe you love a room at your friend's house or at your grandparents' house. No matter what space makes you most happy, it is always so much fun and gratifying to draw a whole room or a portion of a room in your journal.

You can draw a doorway or a window in your favorite room. You can also try drawing your favorite spaces or rooms as if you're looking down on them from above.

DRAW YOUR FAVORITE ROOM OR CORNER OF A ROOM.

FOOD AND DRINK

How can a day on a journal page be filled without some sort of food or drink? Food is an essential part of our days because we need it to live! Drawing food can be incredibly creative and fun. What you choose to eat for a snack, how it tastes, and what it looks like can shape your whole page.

Imagine trying a vegetable for the first time. How can you draw the experience? You can simply draw the vegetable, but you can also draw your face with a smile or a frown based on whether or not you enjoyed it. Small food items can spread across your page to fill empty spaces. You can have strings of pasta stretching from one side of the page to the other. Maybe you had a hot dog with some ketchup and mustard. You can draw the hot dog, or you can think of a more abstract way to draw it. You can paint with yellow and red lines and make drips

with those colors. Drawing your meals, or even the different meals each family member had when you went out to dinner, can take you back to a special birthday or holiday. Food and taste can trigger so many memories! Have fun exploring all the ways you can draw what you eat.

DRAW YOUR FAVORITE MEAL AT YOUR FAVORITE RESTAURANT.

DRAW YOUR FAVORITE SWEET TREAT.

DRAW THE PACKAGE FOR SOMETHING YOU LOVE TO EAT.

DRAW A PATTERN MADE FROM SNACKS OR FOOD THAT COME IN SMALL PIECES.

October 10th 2020

A WOMAN & HER DOG IN FRONT of ME @ BUTLER

WE DRIVE TO SPRINGS FOR 36 HOURS
A WALK ON BEACH @ INDIAN WELLS. DINNER ON BURKES PORCH. ITS WINDY WITH SUNSHINE

PEOPLE

It is hard to draw our days without drawing people, right? Drawing our family and friends will help to make our days on paper more interesting! There are so many ways that you can draw people—from stick figures to very realistic drawings, and everything in between. I encourage you to keep at it, because even if it feels hard, it will get easier. I have been drawing people for years and I still find it challenging. It is important to remember, like with many sections of this book, that however you choose to take on the challenge, your drawings will be uniquely yours. In fact, you can keep drawing stick figures forever if you choose to.

SOME BASIC RULES OF THE HUMAN BODY:

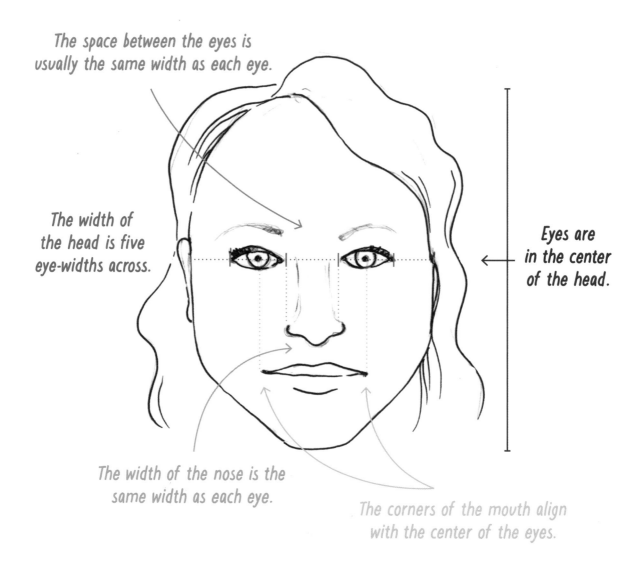

The space between the eyes is usually the same width as each eye.

The width of the head is five eye-widths across.

Eyes are in the center of the head.

The width of the nose is the same width as each eye.

The corners of the mouth align with the center of the eyes.

There are many of these rules, and they are so fun to learn because once you do, you will see people in a whole new way! Look closer at your family members or friends, and you will find that most of these proportions are nearly universal for all people.

If you want to make the people in your journal look more realistic, practice using these rules. That's always the best advice, and if you choose to take your drawing lessons further, you can buy books all about anatomy and the human body.

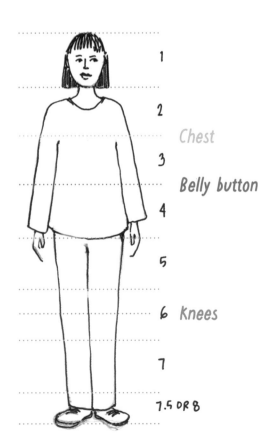

The height of our bodies is approximately 8 heads high!

1

2

Chest

3

Belly button

4

5

6 Knees

7

7.5 OR 8

DRAW TWO OR THREE PEOPLE. Use the body proportion sample I have provided to help you plan the sizes and shapes of the different body parts. You can draw your best friends, your teachers, your doctor, your grandparents, or a stranger you see out in the world who smiled at you or wore an outfit you really liked. Use a photo or ask people to pose for you.

"Have no fear of perfection, you'll never reach it."

~SALVADOR DALÍ

PART FIVE
PUTTING IT ALL TOGETHER

ARRANGING YOUR DRAWINGS ON THE PAGE

Congratulations! You're finally going to put everything together onto the pages of your sketch journal.

Now we're going to explore different ways to combine ideas and visual elements to form a whole, pleasing image.

If you draw lightly in pencil, as we discussed earlier, then you can try several arrangements—erasing and redrawing as needed—before making your finished drawings. There are a couple of things I like to remind my students to do:

1. Use the edges of your page. Make your drawings fall right off the sides just like they do in a photograph. When you take a picture with a camera, the whole frame is filled, so think of your page like a photograph. Having the image bleed off the sides is exciting to the eyes!
2. Vary the size of your drawings, making some big and some little, and have them overlap if you can.

There is no right way to arrange the drawings on your page, but if you think about big and small, and filling all the space on the page, then your artwork will be very inviting and interesting to look at!

COMMON COMPOSITIONS

Here are examples of different compositions. They do not have to be followed exactly, but are meant to inspire you.

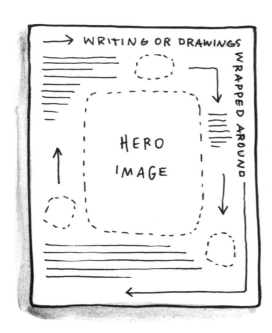

1. **Hero image:** This is a very simple and straightforward composition where you focus on one large image, centered on the page. You can add writing below, on top, or all around.

2. **The Rule of Thirds:** Divide your page into nine even sections (see the dotted lines) in a very light pencil mark. Where two of the lines meet or cross is an area of focus. This is a very popular and useful trick. Have one big thing fall in the area where the lines meet. Then you can build smaller things around.

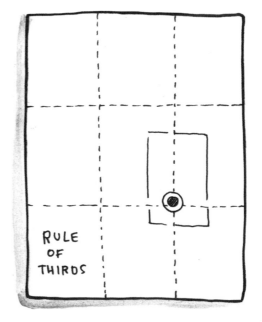

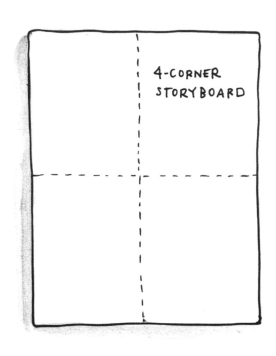

3. **Storyboard:** Divide your page into four even sections lightly in pencil. Have fun telling a four-part story.

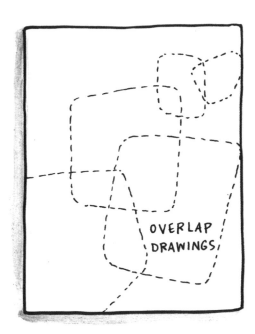

4. **Cascading illustrations:** Start large at the bottom, and have the illustrations or drawings get smaller as they go back in space. Make an effort to lightly sketch various things right on top of one another.

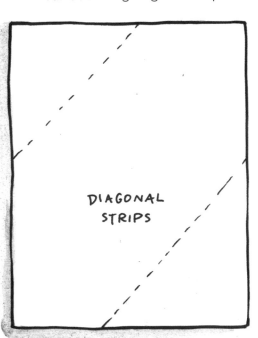

5. **Diagonal strips:** Divide your surface or page into three uneven parts using two diagonal lines. Fill these areas with different colors, patterns, or illustrations.

MAKE YOUR DRAWINGS FALL OFF THE EDGES OF YOUR PAGE

Having your drawing fall right off the edges of your page is very important to creating dynamic compositions. When you take a photograph with a camera, there is color and action filling the entire image. If you take a picture of your friend, for example, she doesn't appear in the middle of white, right? There are things in the background and all around her that fill the whole space of the picture, right off the edges. You do not have to always make your drawings fill the whole page and fall off the edges, but I want you to think about the possibilities, knowing that some or all of your artwork can!

A BANANA
A JUMP ROPE
AND
A SKATEBOARD
ALL FALLING
RIGHT OFF
THE SIDES.

DRAWING CHALLENGE

COMPOSE A PRACTICE IMAGE THAT APPEARS TO FALL OFF THE EDGE OF THE "PAGE." Think of the rectangle below as a page in this sketchbook. Come up with three things to draw, maybe a food item, a toy or stuffed animal you love, and a favorite piece of clothing. Sketch them in the box, making sure one is large and the other two are smaller. Try to have the drawings overlap the dotted outline on at least two of the sides. Once you have a light sketch, erase anything that falls outside the dotted line. Suddenly your drawing will be like photographs, with the images falling right off the sides.

NEGATIVE SPACE AND HOW YOU CAN USE IT

You might find that you have empty space after you put your sketches on your page. Whether your drawings are large or small, the space that they take up is called *positive space,* and the empty surrounding area is called *negative space.* The negative space is the perfect place to add patterns, tiny drawings, the date, or just some writing about how you feel and why you chose to draw what you did on your page. (We will talk more about writing and lettering on page 121.)

The negative space around your drawings is usable and should be considered as you complete your pages. Sometimes it is best to leave the outside space empty or filled with one solid color. This way the focus is on the portraits themselves. But other times, it is fun to fill all that space with smaller drawings and writing. You can have a title or headline above the figures, or fill all the negative space entirely with your written thoughts and memories. Sometimes it is fun to repeat a small drawing to fill empty spaces. Remember the prompt in the food section when I mentioned making a pattern of small food items? Maybe you had M&M's for a snack, or almonds, raisins, or blueberries. You can draw these small images over and over to create balance around your page. You can even have some fall right off the edges.

GRAY AREA: POSITIVE SPACE

WHITE AREA: NEGATIVE SPACE

BLUEBERRIES for T and a PILE OF SCIENCE flashcards on the coffee table

1/26 2018

SUNNY HIGH 35°

EMPIRE STORES HAS BECOME A SECOND OFFICE FOR ME, AS I WAIT TO MOVE INTO THE NEW SPACE JUST A FEW BLOCKS AWAY.

ONE CORTADO

FACETIME WITH M IN ITALY AS HE IS ON WAY TO EAT

Theo home for the 4th day due to a virus. We do 2 rounds of missed school work while I work on this page and we watch "Battle of the Exes"

FEED, Dumbo
@ Empire Stores, Water St.

Example of one of my sketch journal pages with blueberries scattered around the sides

DRAW A LARGE OBJECT, THEN FILL THE EMPTY SPACE AROUND IT. The main object can be a flower, a person, a musical instrument—anything large enough to be the main focus. Then look at the empty area around that drawing. The negative space can form really interesting shapes. What will fill in nicely? Some writing? Smaller drawings? Stripes or polka dots?

LETTERING AND TYPOGRAPHY

At some point you will want to add thoughts and special words to describe an event and to help you remember that day when you look back on the page later. Words are what make this a sketch journal and not just a sketchbook full of random drawings. There are endless creative ways to draw the letters of the alphabet, and there is no wrong way to draw them!

You can write a lot or a little to help describe what you have chosen to draw. On some pages you might want to write more so that you don't forget the details of the day's events. On other pages you might draw just one picture and the date because the image captures the most exciting part of that day. I fill my pages with many different styles of writing—from bubble letters to fancy cursive letters, or a mix of both.

"WE MUST ALWAYS BE ON THE LOOKOUT FOR THE PRESENCE OF WONDER." ~E.B. WHITE

There are pens just for writing and decorative lettering, such as calligraphy pens and brush pens. Learning how to use them fills books and takes a lot of practice. You may want to explore these on your own. But I choose to keep things loose and natural in my sketch journals. I find it easier to use a permanent fine-line pen for everything—drawing special letters and words and regular journal writing.

SUMMER
Solstice
JUNE
21st
2018

FIRST DAY
OF Summer

BRUNO in DUMBO

AUG 6 2017 CAMP PICK-UP DAY

In your journal, you will be writing your thoughts and feelings; therefore, most words will be written in your natural handwriting. There are a lot of things you can do with simple handwriting. You can write one word in all capital letters and the next in lowercase, and alternate each word this way for a few sentences. Or you can alternate uppercase and lowercase when writing one word. You can also go over your letters a few times with your pen to make words bold or write on an angle to make them italicized. I recommend practicing and experimenting to see what you can do with your own handwriting.

Be Silly. Be Honest. Be Kind

I have found that one of the best ways to explore and create really unique lettering is to copy some letters that you see in the world. Once you begin to look for interesting typography, you will spot it everywhere! In your kitchen, on comics and book covers, in magazines, on street signs and postcards. Start to look for the most exciting or unique letters by opening your kitchen cabinets or looking on your bookshelf. Do you spot your initials anywhere? Make a stack of things that inspire you and bring them to your drawing table. Start to copy some of the words or individual letters on your scrap paper. How can you transform them to make them uniquely yours? Maybe you can fill the letters you copy with patterns.

Copying letters that you see out in the world is the best way to learn and explore!

WRITE TODAY'S DATE IN BUBBLE LETTERS, AND THEN USE A DIFFERENT COLOR TO SHADE IN EACH LETTER AND NUMBER. The date is a very important element on your journal pages. When you look back, you will know exactly when something happened and how old you were when you created the entry.

WRITE YOUR NAME, MAKING EACH LETTER A COMPLETELY DIFFERENT STYLE.

Look in magazines or at book covers to find inspiration.

FIND SOME FUN LETTERS AROUND YOUR HOUSE AND PRACTICE COPYING THEM. Look at comic books, magazines, books, sports logos, cereal boxes, toys, or board game boxes for some good ideas.

Saturday, September 1st
LABOR DAY WEEKEND
a little girl with a bucket seen at
Girard Point at 10am

CONCLUSION

There are so many ways to draw your days on paper. From using the colors of your mood to creatively drawing a daily habit to sketching the things right in front of you! The possibilities are endless as long as you open your eyes and look for inspiration around you and within you. Not only are you surrounded by a multitude of things to draw, you can think of countless ways to draw them. It is up to you. My hope is that in the process of exploring and practicing, you will find your own voice as an artist while also capturing memories that you can look back on for years to come.

I am so excited for you to start your own journal. But before you do, come visit me in my studio to see where I work and get to know me a little better.

After that, it will be your turn to find the artist within you and to record your own history in your own sketch journal on page 136!

Remember to have fun!

PART SIX
A VISIT TO MY STUDIO

Photos by Diane Josephine Hu

THANK YOU SO MUCH FOR FOLLOWING ALONG WITH ME THIS FAR!

I have been drawing and doodling for as long as I can remember, but it took a lot of patience and practice to be able to draw in a style that I am happy with. There have been many frustrating moments and countless mistakes along the way.

When I was your age I was surrounded by really talented artists in my family, so I was always comparing my artwork to theirs and never feeling quite good enough. But I was determined to find my own way. As I practiced, the place that I felt most comfortable was in a sketchbook because I could quickly turn the page and start fresh again. And being able to look back and track my progress (and mistakes!) really helped.

This is me in my studio in Brooklyn, New York. On the wall behind me are pages from my own sketch journals that I have scanned and printed out. I like to have them there as a reminder of all the hard work I do each and every day to grow as an artist, a teacher, and a mother.

FLOWERS IN THE STUDIO

As I have gotten older, my sketch journals have become my happy place, almost like a favorite blanket. I now have a stack of sketchbooks so high I can't carry them all! Imagine all the days, memories, and drawing practice that are in these books.

Sharing my process and the things I think about when I create my sketch journal pages with you has been a real gift to me, and I am thankful and excited that you joined me on this creative journey.

If you'd like to see more of my journal pages, visit my Instagram:
@SDIONBAKERDESIGN

If you would like to learn more about me
and the projects I am working on, please visit my website:
SDIONBAKER.COM

STACK OF MY ALL-FILLED UP SKETCHBOOKS

Start YOUR journal here

Now it's time for you to begin your own sketch journal adventure. So start a new page . . . and Draw Your Day!